Don Aslett's Clean *In A* Minute

Don Aslett

Illustrated by Craig LaGory

Dedication

    To all you folks out there who have called, written, visited me and even prayed for a faster, easier, cheaper and more fun way to clean...
this book is for you!

Don Aslett's
Clean
In A Minute

Table of Contents

Clean
In A
Minute.

Yes...
Just a Minute

It was mid term in a college course I was teaching, for forty students being trained for the cleaning and maintenance industry. Painting was one of the subjects we had to cover, and today was the day. Groans, hisses and boos greeted my announcement of the subject: "I hate to paint," "It takes forever," "I can't even stand the smell of the stuff," "The only thing I've ever painted is my nails"...

Painting is unquestionably a negative for a lot of people, and to make matters worse, I'd secured an empty rental house near the college, which I informed them we were going to paint as we learned... more moans. One student, who was familiar with the home in question, said "That place will take the rest of the year." The class cheered his analysis,

hoping we'd just skip the subject and move on to upholstery cleaning. My son Grant was helping me teach this summer session (he'd been a professional painter since the age of eight). He'd also seen the home, and to save me from being stoned, he stood up and said: "I could paint the entire master bedroom in 30 minutes... alone." He'd performed previous cleaning miracles for the class and so all were silent and all were anxious to see this "two-day" room job done in half an hour.

The room was a large one, but we'd prepared it the day before, and it was a modern home so it had low ceilings, no woodwork, and only one door. And the paint we'd be using was pretty close to what was on there already (the easiest of all painting). The students crowded around to watch and Grant, armed with the most modern and best professional equipment, spread his dropcloths, and with pinpoint neatness and never a spill or drip or splash, did indeed knock the room out in 25 minutes. Then, because everyone had made such an issue of how they hated the cleanup after painting most of all, he cleaned up everything— roller, brushes, buckets, and trays, in 7 minutes more. All of the onlookers were suddenly believers... yes, maybe **minutes** could do something.

Likewise, in the early days of my cleaning company, a woman led me to a long dark stairwell off her kitchen. It was steep and scary looking and she hadn't cleaned it in eight years, so it was dirty. But it was also a hard-surface high-quality enamel finish, so it was a piece of cake for someone who knew how to ladder and plank it (see page 50). So I put my extension ladder on the bottom basement step, my stepladder on the entrance landing, and a plank across the steps—it only took 5 minutes to set it up. Now that the hard part was done, getting in position to reach what had to be cleaned, there was very little square footage to clean. So in 10 minutes the whole stairwell was sparkling and beautiful, and as a bonus I took down, cleaned, and replaced the ceiling light too. She'd waited years, and IT ONLY TOOK MINUTES.

Another time, we got a call from a 76-year-old man who'd always done the floor in his kitchen. Now he was a little arthritic, so he was seeking help at last from the professionals. He'd blanked a whole day out for the job because that was how long it usually took him. It was a good size floor, but we laid down some good strong commercial stripper, worked it over with a little nylon pad on a long-handled floor scrubber (see p. 38), and in 5 minutes all the ancient dirt and wax was released from the surface. Then in just 20 SECONDS more we squeegeed all the old wax into a puddle in the middle of the room, and scooped it up in another 20 seconds. One more MINUTE and it was damp mopped. The elderly gentleman gasped in disbelief seeing these new tools and techniques, and decided he could do the floor himself for at least another decade. And so he has, and it only takes him MINUTES, smiling all the while.

The wall at the end of the living room was another homeowner's pride and joy, it was covered with wallpaper well dirtied by smoke and time. She'd fretted over it forever, and finally called my company to clean it. When I looked at the wall and told her it would only

TAKE A MINUTE to clean, she laughed. I whipped out one of the dry sponges (see p. 53) we professionals use (like a giant eraser) on fire damage jobs and it cleaned that wall wonderfully, and yes, it only took me 60 seconds to do it...

I could share hundreds of other stories with you, of how quickly and easily even the grungiest cleaning jobs can be done using the methods, the tools, and the materials of the professionals. You need this now more than ever because the full days we once had to do household jobs and chores— washday, ironing day, baking day, cleaning day—have almost disappeared from our lives. Nowadays we often don't even get hours for things like this, we get MINUTES, minutes before, after, in between, and during our many other involvements and responsibilities. We do it fast, or we don't get another chance to do it. So I've covered the common cleaning chores in this convenient book. It compresses forty years of professional shortcuts into just a few pages, shows you exactly what to use and how to do it. You'll enjoy this graphic and easy-to-use manual. It works and will only take **MINUTES** to read!

Why Clean?

Before getting to the nitty-gritty of what to do and how to do it, I'd like to give you three good reasons to clean:

1 It makes us look and feel good

Neat, clean, orderly surroundings don't just give us a feeling of peace and control, they're easier to function in. We aren't constantly looking for and stumbling over things. Cleaning cuts down on household irritations and arguments, too. And best of all it carries over into our overall confidence and self-esteem so we can go out into the world and make a mark!

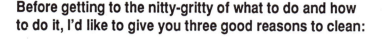

2 It helps us stay healthy

Cleaning eliminates the germs that cause disease and odors, and the dirt and debris that attract insects and other pests. And it saves us from falls and other accidents caused by clutter.

3 It saves money

A little preventive maintenance keeps away the dirt that plugs up and stops things from working. When carpets, flooring, upholstery, clothes, etc. are allowed to stay dirty they develop permanent stains and wear out before their time. The people who use them will hasten the process, too, by starting to abuse them "because they already look so bad."

If you'd like to know more about why we clean, see *The Cleaning Encyclopedia.*

Preventing Cleaning

... the biggest pro secret of all!

80% of the dirt in your house comes in on people and pets—tracked in. The solution—stop it in its tracks. Keep the dirt out! The most effective way is with the right kind of mats at all your entrances.

Good mats will catch all the grit and gravel before it gets in and scratches and wears out your floors. They'll pull off the soil and tar, etc. before it gets embedded in your carpet. And they absorb rainwater, slush, road salt, and mud.

Mats save tons of cleaning time and energy, save cleaning supplies and wear and tear on your cleaning equipment as well as your home and its furnishings.

Once you have mats you won't have to vacuum or shampoo your carpets as much, or sweep, scrub, strip, and wax your floors as often. Mats reduce dusting, too, and keep clothes, drapes, and upholstery cleaner.

They make your entrances safer, quieter, and better looking, too.

I'm not talking about little rubber mats with daisies on them, or tire link or coco mats, or carpet squares you scrounged from somewhere. Forget them—they're ineffective, and dangerous, too.

The mats I mean are professional "walkoff" mats, like the ones you've seen at the entrances of supermarkets, department stores, and hospitals. You can get them at janitorial-supply stores, or by mail from The Cleaning Center.

For inside the door you want nylon or olefin with rubber or vinyl backing.

For outside the door you want rubber or vinyl backed artificial turf. To do a good job of dirt catching both the inside and outside mats need to be at least 4 strides long. Choose 2'x3', 3'x4', or 3'x5' if there's room!

If you have an entrance from the garage, be sure to mat it too. A lot of nasty stuff works its way into the house from there.

For more ways to use mats to prevent housework, see *Is There Life After Housework!*

To maintain mats:

1 Keep them vacuumed.

2 Every so often, hose and scrub away the dirt.

3 Squeegee off the water with a floor squeegee.

4 Hang until completely dry before putting them back down. Never use when back is wet.

Sealing...

Or making it impossible for dirt to penetrate. When you seal you apply a (usually clear) coating to something that protects it from soil, stains, and moisture. Sealing also fills the pores and smooths the surface, so it's a lot easier to clean when it finally does need it. Sealing will also stop dust from bleeding off things like concrete.

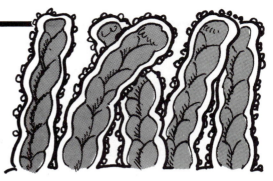

Soil Retardant forms an "invisible shield" around the fibers of your carpet.

What should I seal it with?

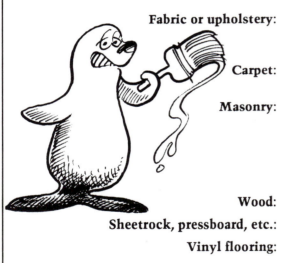

Sealers can be sprayed, rolled, brushed, mopped, or wiped on, and once they're good and dry you're in business.

Fabric or upholstery: Soil retardant such as Scotchgard. It can even be applied at the store or factory like "Soil Shield."

Carpet: Soil retardant such as Carpet Guard or 3M Carpet Protector.

Masonry: (brick, stone, concrete, terrazzo, etc.) Masonry seal (your local masonry can advise you of precisely the right one for the surface or material you have in mind). The newer water-based ones are best.

Wood: Polyurethane, varnish, shellac, etc.

Sheetrock, pressboard, etc.: Enamel paint.

Vinyl flooring: Floor finish or "wax."

Sealing Secrets

1. Seal it now, while it's fresh and clean and new. If you wait a few months or a few years, you'll have to do a major cleanup first, and many stains may be impossible to get out.

2. Several light coats are usually better than one thick one, when you're applying sealer.

3. Sealers don't last forever—you need to reapply them when they wear off from use; or whenever you deep clean (wash or shampoo) the article.

> **Read more about it in *The Cleaning Encyclopedia, Is There Life After Housework!* and *Make Your House Do The Housework*.**

A Few Other Preventive Measures

Prepare! Remember that the mess is coming, and take steps to minimize it. We're always anxious to get on with the job, we never want to take the time to bother with this, but do put down that dropcloth, spread those old newspapers, move that armchair. It only takes a fraction of the time it'll take to remove all the stains, drips, and splashes otherwise.

☑ **Become aware of, and break, all those mess-making habits,** from turning the frying pan on too high to pouring things so fast they always spill all over.

☑ **Confine smoking** to certain easy-to-clean areas, or move it outdoors.

☑ **Make sure house animals are housebroken** (and don't expect anything but cats to teach themselves).

☑ **Seal** anything that stains or absorbs dirt too easily.

☑ **If it's an impossible to clean surface,** cover or refinish it, paint or paper or panel it.

☑ **Make sure your vacuum isn't leaking** dust back into the air (are the bag seals tight?).

☑ **Keep your furnace and air conditioner filters** cleaned and changed. This will do a lot to cut down airborne dirt.

☑ **Close up cracks and crevices** around windows and doors and in the foundation, to keep out dust, moisture, and pests.

☑ **Consider a central vac,** home extractor, electrostatic air cleaner, dishwasher, garbage disposal, or compactor—whatever cleaning machinery will make the work go better and faster and make your life easier. It'll do more to brighten your life than expensive seldom-used "toys."

Design Cleaning Out

Cleaning faster and more efficiently is fine, but why not go one better and simply ELIMINATE all the cleaning you can? Build, remodel, and design it out.

A lot of our housework headaches are caused by the fact that the people who design and build our homes and furnishings aren't usually the ones who have to maintain them. So **we** have to wrestle every day with things that aren't just dirty, but hard or impossible to clean.

You can change that, not only when you remodel or draft your dream house, but every time you buy new carpeting or drapes, furniture or appliances, every time you repaint or redecorate.

Here are some principles of maintenance-freeing design to keep in mind:

☑ **Camouflage It**: Choose colors and textures in your flooring, wall coverings, and furniture that downplay the dirt, fallout, and spills till you have a chance to go after them. Get an orange couch if you have an orange cat.

☑ **Suspend It**: If you can get it up off the floor or counter, do so—it'll take up less space, won't collect dirt under it, and won't get in your way when you're cleaning. Suspend those small appliances, tables, chairs, lamps, coat racks, etc.

☑ **Build It In**: Built-in furniture and appliances, for example, save not only space but bumps and grazes on you and the furnishings, and eliminate a lot of sides, backs, and underneaths to clean.

☑ **Keep It Simple**: The less details and decorations, the less curves, joints, grooves, edges, and ledges, the fewer kinds of materials it's made of, the

Some Time Robbers to Avoid

- **Indented or embossed tile or floor covering.** It looks great but recessed surfaces collect dirt, are hard to sweep, and will gradually fill with wax.

- **Indoor-outdoor carpet.** It shows every crumb or speck of lint. It's difficult to clean and adds zero plushness to a home.

- **Highly textured walls and ceilings.** They hold dirt and are a dust and cobweb paradise. They're hard to clean and paint.

- **Unfinished wood. Looks** nice and rustic, but once it's soiled, you've had it. Wood should always be sealed with a resinous or polyurethane finish.

- **Fancy hardware.** This takes time to keep up and provides breeding grounds for germs.

- **Extremely high ceilings.** Although it's impressive to have a couple of 25- to 30-foot ceilings in your house, they're hard to maintain and energy-wasteful.

- **Multi-surface furniture and fixtures.** Every surface needs maintenance—so the less surface the better. Eliminate ledges and wedges where possible. A louvered door, for example, has much more surface than a simple, smooth door. Likewise, furnishings or walls made of many different materials take more time and types of equipment to clean.

- **Dark colors.** Whether furniture, floors, or countertops, dark colors require more daily upkeep than medium-colored items (dark colors show dust and spots—everything!).

- **Decoration clusters.** One nice big picture sure beats a clump of thirty-two dusty little ones (and cheats spiders out of bases).

easier it will be to clean, and keep clean. And the less equipment and supplies you'll need to do it.

☑ **Choose the Smooth**: Anything with an uneven, indented or relief-design surface—from floor covering to countertop material to wall covering—is going to accumulate dirt faster and be harder to clean.

☑ **Keep it in Reach—Your Reach**: Forget about what's standard or usual or customary. Make sure it's not too high or too low or inaccessible—for you.

☑ **Foil Airborne Grease and Soil**: We rarely think about it or see it happening, but this quiet aerial invasion is one of the biggest mess-makers we have to contend with. Choose heating, cooking, and ventilation systems accordingly and consider an electrostatic air cleaner.

☑ **Avoid High-Maintenance Materials**: Anything that needs constant polishing or servicing, that stains or damages easily, or shows every sand grain or lint speck immediately.

> The chart above is from my book *Make Your House Do The Housework*, (Copyright 1986 used with permission).
>
> I teamed up with my daughter (an interior designer) to write this step-by-step guide to applying maintenance-freeing design to every room in your house. Hundreds of hassle and labor-saving ideas you can start taking advantage of today. You'll find it in your bookstore or library, or you can order it by mail on page 65.

Get Help!

WELL, I'M GONNA CALL IT A DAY! THE LITTLE WOMAN'S CALLIN' ME HOME TO SWEEP OUT THE TEEPEE.

Another good way of preventing cleaning is to prevent it from all being done by you—GET HELP.

Keeping things clean and appealing isn't all your problem, even if that's the impression everyone's had forever. A lot of the feeling that housework is "hopeless" is a result of the fact that for all too long 90% of the housework has been created by men and children, and 90% of it done by MOM.

You don't want to be the family janitor—it's not only hard on you, it's bad for everyone involved. When you constantly clean up behind people you teach them that they're not responsible for their own messes, that someone is always going to come after them and tidy up... a bad attitude that carries over into other even more important parts of life. (It contributes mightily to the litter on our sidewalks and roadsides, too.)

If they're old enough to mess up, they're old enough to clean up. It's amazing how much faster cleanup goes when several pairs of hands are doing it, not just one, when you divide the work by two, or three, or five.

An eager woman at my seminar picked up a copy of my little book *Who Says It's A Woman's Job To Clean?* (the one that gets men and boys to do their share of the housework).

"Will it work?" she asked, thumbing through the pages.

"Well," my wife answered, "there are a lot of proven, easy-to-follow directions in there and they all work. If the men at your house end up only doing **one** of those things, but do it for the rest of their lives...."

A light came into the woman's eyes, "I'll take six of them, please."

Sources of Help

Men (don't let them kid you, they're just as capable of performing the motions involved as women, if not more so—remember, most pro cleaners are men).

Teenagers (of either sex) who are full-scale people, though possibly not always recognizable as such during this period of their lives. Point out that the ability to clean fast, well, and cheerfully will do more than bigger biceps or bosoms to make them more attractive to potential mates.

Children over the age of 3. It's never too soon to start teaching neatness, self-reliance, and consideration for others.

Guests always ask if they can help, so just stop turning them down. They'll feel more comfortable and you won't be so exhausted you can't enjoy their company.

Professional cleaners are available for all kinds of pro assistance, from maid service to specialized cleaning contractors of all kinds. You only have to pick up a phone to have help with big seasonal heavy-duty jobs or everyday keep-up cleaning. If you can afford outside help (check it out, it may not cost as much as you think), don't hesitate to use it.

Do Unto Mother as you do at McDonald's.

Licking Household Litter

Half of all housework is **straightening up** (putting things back like they were or back where they belong), and **handling household litter** (dropped trash and left behind possessions). The worst part is that when you're done, you're only where you should have been when you started. Litter causes fights, arguments, and resentments too, plus people can't find their stuff (jackets, books, pocketknives, etc.) when they need it.

THE NUMBER ONE SOLUTION is a simple rule:

1 Everyone picks up after themselves. Once you make that rule, stick with it—don't just shrug your shoulders and give up if people don't seem to be remembering it right away. Behavior and tradition take time to change. It may take some doing, but once you've taught them your life will be different—BETTER—forever after.

A couple of other things that will help:

2 Make sure there's A PLACE TO PUT IT and there's a much better chance it'll be put away. Provide drawers, hooks, pegboards, shelves, toyboxes that they don't have to go far to find. Great Truth of Human Nature #242: If it's easy to do, they might do it.

3 Make sure there's a PLACE TO GET RID OF IT. Put convenient, visible waste containers not only in every room, but in the yard and the garage.

Junk & Clutter:
Get rid of it!

Which would you rather clean!

Cut Your Housework in Half:

What is Junk? All that "stuff" you aren't using, don't really want, don't need, don't enjoy, and don't have room for!

At least **40%** of what we call "house-cleaning" is just junk tending—not just dusting and polishing it, but keeping track of it, storing it, insuring it, protecting it, organizing and reorganizing it, repositioning it.

Cluttered rooms take 10X or more the time to clean, because we have to move so much out of the way to do anything, and then move it all back when we're done. And all those extra objects add up to hundreds of times the amount of surface to clean. You also need many more kinds of equipment and supplies to clean them.

Junk wastes our time and makes us inefficient, steals our love and affection, and stops us from getting to the things we really care about in life. It boggles our minds as well as our storage areas.

DEJUNK—start today. It's the shortest path to household freedom. It doesn't cost a cent to do and it will even save you money.

Dejunk—toss it, trade it, tromp it, give it away, sell it— but get rid of it. It'll be the greatest housework reducing move you ever make. The formula is easy:

Don't love anything that can't love you back.
If something doesn't enhance your life then part with it. When? Now, today. I can promise that dejunking will change your life (and housework schedule) more than any other single thing you can do.

If you need more convincing than this, see *Clutter's Last Stand.* For a step-by-step guide on how to dejunk, see *Not For Packrats Only.*

Head out to those Junk Havens:	Tackle the Top Troublemakers:
Closets	Clothes
Drawers	Papers
Desks	Containers and
Shelves	Packaging
Attics	Sentimental Stuff
Basements	Gadgets
Backyards	Grooming Aids
Storage Bins	Hobby and Sports
Lockers	Junk
Garages	Excess Furniture
Car Trunks	Gifts and
Porches	Souvenirs
Sheds	Toys
Medicine	Scraps
Cabinets	Stuff to be fixed or
Purses	finished someday

The
Tools
I'll be talking about in this book

These are the tools the professionals use. I introduced them to the home-maker in 1981, and you couldn't tear them away now. It's easy to understand why. They do a faster and better job, and cost less in the long run, too.

Where can you get them? Where the pros do—at the janitorial-supply store. Just look in the Yellow Pages under "J." If you'd find it easier to order them by mail, send a **postcard** with your name and address to Clean Report, PO Box 700, Pocatello, ID 83204 and they'll be happy to send you a catalog.

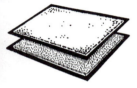

Mats. Professional "walkoff" mats for inside and outside the door. **Inside** you want nylon or olefin pile with vinyl or rubber backing. **Outside** you want something more textured such as synthetic turf on a nonskid backing. 3' x 5' or 3' x 6' is a good size.

Spray Bottle. Sturdy transparent plastic with a trigger-spray head. Pro-quality spray bottles perform better and last longer and come in 22 oz. and quart size.

Neutral All-Purpose Cleaner. A gentle but effective cleaner that will handle most of the household cleaning we do. Available as concentrate in gallon jugs or premeasured packets.

Heavy-Duty Cleaner/Degreaser. A meaner cleaner for when you're up against greasy or stubborn soil. Available as concentrate in gallon jugs or premeasured packets.

Glass Cleaner. The pro version of a "Windex" type cleaner you can mix up yourself inexpensively from concentrate. For spray cleaning small window-panes, mirrors, appliances, chrome. Available in gallon jugs or premeasured packets.

Disinfectant Cleaner. A general-purpose cleaner with serious germ-killing ability, for anyplace in the home that needs sanitizing or deodorizing. A "quaternary" is the kind you want. Available as concentrate.

White Nylon Scrub Sponge. A regular cellulose sponge on one side, white nylon mesh on the other. My all-around favorite cleaning tool. Enables you to get tough with dirt whenever you need to as you're cleaning along, without taking a chance of scratching things. 3M makes a good one.

Cleaning Cloth. The pro cleaner's secret weapon, for quick streak-free drying, polishing, wiping, and mild scrubbing. Made from cotton terrycloth in an ingenious design that gives you 16 fresh surfaces to work with. See p. 23 for how to make your own; also available from The Cleaning Center.

Bucket. Professional-strength plastic such as the Rubbermaid Brute is best—it won't scratch or leave rust stains anywhere and it's quieter, too. Plastic buckets are even available in a diamond shape now, that will fit squeegee and sponge mop heads and is easier to pour and carry.

Dust Mop. You want a 14" or 18" pro model with a cotton head and a swivel handle.

Damp Mop. Either a pro-quality sponge mop (janitorial-supply stores will have these) with replaceable head or a 12 or 16 oz. pro-quality wet mop with a rayon/cotton head.

Long-handled Floor Scrubber. Such as a Scrubbee Doo or Doodlebug. Tools like these have interchangeable pads with different degrees of "scrub" as well as wax applicator and dustmop heads. You won't believe how much easier this makes not only floor scrubbing and stripping but cleaning shower walls and house siding, etc.

Wax Stripper. Commercial strength, nonammoniated.

"Wax" or Floor Finish. A "22-25% solid, self-polishing, non-buffable" such as Top Gloss.

Upright Vacuum. For speed, maneuverability and pickup power on carpeting, these can't be beat. A commercial model such as the Eureka Sanitaire has a stronger motor, beater bar and bag, a longer cord, and more durable and easily replaceable parts all over.

17

Masslinn Cloth. A disposable paper "cloth" that's chemically treated to catch and hold dust. It also leaves a nice non-oily low luster on furniture.

Electrostatic Dustcloth. Dustcloths such as the Dust Bunny and New Pig made of special fabric that attracts and holds dust by static electricity. When they're laden with dust they can be laundered and reused.

Lambswool Duster. A large puff of wool on a long handle, that does high and low dusting with ease. You can also run it across detailed and convoluted surfaces like fancy picture frames, woodwork, and bookcases, and it will reach in and gently pull off the dust without disturbing anything. The natural oil and static attraction of the wool is the secret.

Dust Treat. A (usually oily) preparation applied to dustmops and dustcloths to help them capture and hold dust. Available as aerosols such as Endust and as a liquid that you put in your own spray bottle. Follow the directions faithfully and you'll see why the pros wouldn't dustmop without it.

Oil Soap. A true soap (as opposed to the detergents we mostly clean with today) made from vegetable oil. It's mild enough to clean wood surfaces safely, and the little bit of oil it leaves behind on the surface will be buffed by your drying towel to a handsome sheen.

Squeegee. To do a first-class job you need a pro-quality brass squeegee such as the Ettore. A 12" blade is best for most home size windows; for picture windows and the like you might want to go to 14" or larger.

Window Scrubber. A T-shaped tool covered with fleece, used to apply cleaning solution to windows and degrime them as necessary. On an extension handle it makes short work of high windows.

Extension Handle. The safer, easier way to extend your reach when cleaning. Available in 8 and 12-foot lengths that telescope down to 4' for storage. They're made of aluminum or fiberglass for lightness and can be used with squeegees, window wands, lambswool dusters, and paint rollers.

Bowl Swab with bowl caddy. A "bunny tail" of cotton, rayon, or acrylic on a plastic handle. Used for applying bowl cleaner to a toilet, and for coaxing all of the water out of the bowl first so the cleaner can work full strength.

Phosphoric Acid Cleaner. For removing mineral or "lime" scale. The 8 or 9% solution you can get at janitorial-supply stores (you don't want anything stronger than that for home use) will work much faster than supermarket delimers.

Pumice Stone. A small block of pumice (hardened froth from volcano lava!) used to "sand" away stubborn raised rings in the toilet.

Dry Sponge. A disposable 5" x 7" pad of soft rubber used to "dry clean" surface dirt and smoke from painted walls, paneling, ceilings, wallpaper, etc.

Bacteria/Enzyme Digester. A culture of live, beneficial bacteria that you mix up to digest organic materials like vomit and urine that cause persistent and hard to remove stains and odors. Outright Pet Odor Eliminator is one good brand.

Pet Rake. A tool specially designed to deal with the exasperating problem of pet hair everywhere. The crimped nylon bristles do an amazing job of getting it up and off upholstered furniture, bedding, car interiors, carpeting, and clothing. Available only from The Cleaning Center.

To receive a catalog with these and other great professional cleaning products, send a **postcard** with your name and address to:
Clean Report
PO Box 700
Pocatello, ID 83204.

Full details on these and the whole universe of professional cleaning products can be found in *The Cleaning Encyclopedia* and *Is There Life After Housework?*

The Basic Principles of Cleaning

$\square = ph \ of \ \frac{1}{2}$

$E = 3 H_2O$

Which will not only save you a lot of work, but prevent damage to your household furnishings and surfaces, and save on cleaning supplies, too.

Let The Chemicals Do the Work

Whenever possible (in fact most of the time), we clean by chemical action, not brute force—see page opposite. Never scrub when you can soak.

Us the Gentlest Product or Approach First

Don't automatically reach for the heavy-duty cleaner or the bleach bottle. Use neutral cleaner and a gentle touch first, and only if that doesn't work move up to something stronger.

Avoid Abrasives Whenever You Can

Such as old-style powdered cleansers, steel wool and harsh (green, brown, etc.,) scrub pads. Things like these literally grind and sand away the surface of your sinks, tubs, counters, floors, etc. and leave them rough and porous. Which means they'll collect dirt faster and be a lot harder to clean in the future.

Identify the Soil First

So you can be sure to use the right chemical. Most soils are water-based, which is why we use a water solution to remove them. But some soils (such as tar, wax, and many adhesives) call for an oil-based solvent to remove them.

pH is important, too.

We all heard about pH back in high school—the measure of how acid or alkaline something is. The scale goes from 1 to 14, and 7, the middle, is neutral. Alkaline things neutralize acids, and vice versa. Many household soils are slightly acid, which is why most cleaning products are alkaline. Acid soils include grease, oil, most body fluids, and many foods.

A few household soils are alkaline and call for an acid cleaner—the most common ones we run into are hard water mineral buildup ("lime scale") and rust.

The stronger the cleaner, the higher the pH—heavy-duty cleaners and degreasers are quite alkaline, 10 or 12 on the pH scale, to help them dissolve heavy grease and stubborn soil. And wax strippers are very "hot"—13-14 or even higher. Both high and low pH cleaners have to be used carefully to prevent damage to you and your household surfaces.

Neutral cleaner is what you can and should use for most general and light-duty cleaning. As the name hints, it's neither acid nor alkaline, but neutral.

The Smart Way to Clean Anything

The quickest, easiest, most efficient way to clean anything that's safe to use water on.

Clean with your head, not your hands. Let the chemicals do the work.

1. Eliminate

Remove all the loose stuff you can first—with a broom, brush, vacuum, scraper, or whatever.

3. Dissolve

Leave the solution on there till it dissolves the dirt. This is a lot easier and safer than rubbing and scrubbing.

2. Saturate

Mix up some cleaning solution and wet down the surface well with it.

4. Remove

Now you can just wipe away all the softened and loosened dirt.

Simplify Your Cleaning Closet

Instead of a whole under-sink arsenal of cleaning liquids, powders, and pastes, boxes, cans, and bottles (half of which you've forgotten you have), all you need are a few professional products. These will not only do a faster and better job, they're cheaper, and easier and safer to use and store. They're also easier on your household surfaces and furnishings and mean less containers to be disposed of.

Why be a water hauler?
Use concentrated cleaners

Most of the cleaners you buy in the supermarket are "ready to use" or highly diluted. Which means they're mostly water. Why pay for, and lug around, all that water?

When you buy professional cleaning chemicals they're in concentrated form—you add your own water at home, just mix up a spray bottle or a bucketful of cleaner and you're ready to go.

Concentrated cleaners are available in bulk such as gallon jugs, and premeasured into little plastic envelopes. The packets prevent waste and wrong dilution, and they're even easier to transport and store (and reduce container trash even more). Just snip and mix!

All you need is four basic cleaners

Neutral All-Purpose Cleaner

Neither acid nor alkaline, so it's safe for almost any surface. A mild but effective cleaner for most everyday household cleaning.

Heavy-Duty Cleaner/Degreaser

A high-pH cleaner with strong dirt-dissolving action for the tough and greasy jobs.

Glass Cleaner

A fast-evaporating alcohol-based cleaner for when you need a streak-free shine: small windows, mirrors, chrome, appliance fronts.

Disinfectant Cleaner

A cleaner that also has disinfecting action, for areas and surfaces that need sanitizing, like the bathroom, sickroom, garbage cans, etc. A "quaternary" is the kind you want, the safest and best for home use.

Now... get yourself some spray bottles

4 or 5 professional-strength plastic "trigger spray" bottles from a janitorial-supply store. They're available in quart (32 oz.) size and will work better and last longer than what you get at the discount or garden store. Get the transparent ones so you can tell what's in them at a glance. And the minute you fill them, label them with permanent marker.

Always MEASURE, don't "glug and guess." We all think we can eyeball it, but even the pros need to read the directions and measure. More isn't better—it doesn't just waste cleaner (and money). It dulls and streaks the surface (can even damage it), will actually make the solution LESS able to dissolve and suspend dirt. It calls for extra rinsing, which wastes water, too.

SPRAY BOTTLE SAVVY

*   *When mixing a spray bottle of cleaner, put the water in first, then add the concentrate. This prevents a four-inch head of foam and dangerous chemical splashes.*
*   *Don't forget that spray bottle nozzles are adjustable, from a fine mist to a thin stream.*
*   *When in doubt (that your aim is good enough to keep the solution where you intended) spray the cleaner onto a cloth and wipe with the cloth.*

> **For more on your basic cleaning arsenal, concentrated cleaners, and how to make good use of spray bottles, see *Is There Life After Housework!***

Professional Cleaning Cloths

(Far better than a "Rag," for cleaning)

There's no doubt that in cleaning a cloth is often the best tool for the job, but the "rags" homemakers hoard and use for this just aren't up to it. They're linty, full of seams, buttons, zippers, and holes, and worst of all often made of materials that fail to absorb or even repel water. Rags like these are fine for cleaning your hands when you're painting, period.

What you need is a supply of the cloths professionals use, for wiping, streak-free drying, buffing, dusting. They're made of cotton terrycloth so they're ultra absorbent, and all the little "nubs" on the terry cloth not only dry things fast but can reach down into textured surfaces. Terry is strong enough to protect your hands while you're working with it on tough jobs, too.

Here's how to make them. Get some heavy cotton terrycloth, preferably white (old towels are fine for the purpose) and cut it into 18"x18" squares. Hem all the edges of each square and fold it over once. Then sew the long side together firmly and you'll have a "tube" of terry. Fold it once, and then again, and it'll just fit your hand. As you use it, it can be folded and refolded and then turned inside out to give you 16 fresh sides to clean with.

When you finish with your cloths, don't just toss them in a pile somewhere and leave them or they'll get stiff and stained. Run them through the washer and then tumble them dry and they'll be ready to work wonders for you again when you need them.

18"

18"

Fold finished cloth to fit your hand, aprox. 4" x 9".

Two-Bucket Cleaning

Shown here washing walls, this method can be applied to any surfaces you wash with liquid cleaner—counters, tables, appliances, entryways, bathroom surfaces—nearly everything. You can also apply cleaner with a spray bottle.

bucket half-filled with cleaner

empty bucket

sponge

cleaning cloth(s)

Dip the sponge about a half-inch into the cleaner

1 Apply the cleaner: Start at the top (or back) and spread the cleaner over an area the size of a comfortable arm's reach.

2 Let it work: Give the cleaner time to dissolve the soil.

3 Remove the dirty cleaner: Go back over the wet area with your sponge, or the white nylon side of a scrub sponge if needed, to dislodge and remove the dirt.

4 Dry the surface: Wipe the sponged area with a folded cleaning cloth.

5 Get rid of the dirt: Squeeze (don't wring) the dirty sponge into the empty bucket.

Now start again: dip the sponge a half-inch into the clean solution and repeat.

When you're finished the empty bucket will be full of dirty water. Your cleaning solution will stay clean and clear.

Dust First!

The average home accumulates 40 pounds of this pesky stuff a year!

Your whole goal here is to **capture and remove** the dust, not just redistribute it. This means you want one of the following tools, depending on what you can get your hands on and what you're dusting:

• a disposable dustcloth such as the Masslinn, or
• an electrostatic dustcloth such as the Dust Bunny or New Pig (see p. 18)
• a lambswool duster, especially good for high or low dusting, knickknacks, and convoluted surfaces
• a vacuum dust brush

No Matter What You Use:

1. Dust before you vacuum.
2. Dust top to bottom, so you don't have to re-dust anything.
3. Dust with a smooth wiping motion, don't whip and flick your tool (and the dust!) around.
4. Turn your cloth or duster over to a clean side as soon as it gets loaded up, and shake it out or replace it before you start spreading dust rather than collecting it.

Don't use furniture polish every time you dust—it just builds up into a sticky, streaky coating that attracts dust.

Your dusting schedule depends a lot on how houseproud you are, and whether or not you're allergic to dust, but some good general guidelines are:

Weekly: the furniture and a whole-house once over lightly.

Monthly: Door frames, woodwork, blinds, drapes, valances, light fixtures, lampshades, de-cobweb, upholstered furniture (don't think it doesn't collect dust).

Twice Yearly: rafters, exposed beams, grills and vents, walls, ceilings.

Prevention makes a lot of sense here:

• Install good walkoff mats at all entrances (see p.6).
• Replace or clean your furnace and air conditioner filters when you should.
• See that cracks and holes leading outside are caulked or weather-stripped.
• Make sure your vacuum isn't leaking dust.
• And that all raw concrete floors are sealed (see p. 8).

For more on dust, dusting technique, and dust control, see *Is There Life After Housework!*

How to Clean
Furniture

Get good quality whenever you can—(bearing in mind the maintenance-freeing principles on p. 10) it keeps its looks longer, is more repairable, and easier to clean. Then if it has a fabric finish, don't put plastic covers on it—Scotchgard it! Now for the particulars:

Wood with a sealed (varnished, etc.) finish. *Dusting* Don't use furniture polish every time you dust—this just builds an oily, sticky coating that attracts dust. Use a Masslinn cloth or electrostatic dustcloth (see p. 18).

For *fingerprints or smudges*, do what the pros do—take a cloth lightly damp-ened with neutral cleaner solution or plain water and wipe them away. Buff right afterward with a dry cloth.

Polish only occasionally and lightly and stick with the same polish—mixing different types will cause streaking.

Furniture with a sealed finish can be *washed* if it's really dirty. Put a plastic sheet or dropcloth all around it and wash with a mild neutral cleaner or oil soap solution, using the two-bucket system (see p. 24), quickly polish it dry.

Raw or oil-finished wood. Should never be wet—only damp-wiped when it needs it. Bare or oil-finished wood needs to be treated periodically with an oil or wood treatment made just for this purpose to keep it from drying out and cracking. Apply it, rub it in, leave it on a while, then blot up the excess.

Upholstered Furniture. Can hide the dirt for quite a while, so we tend to just ignore it. But it needs regular care too. Especially the "trouble zones"—head-rest, armrests, and seat where the human hide meets the Naughahyde.

Upholstery is by no means exempt from the dust that settles on everything indoors. If you leave it on there it'll just combine with skin and hair oil into a hard-to-remove slick. Vacuum weekly at least in the trouble zones to keep dust down. On nondelicate upholstery, you can put your upright right up on the seat cushions to let the beater brush work out embedded dirt.

Before you do anything beyond dusting, read the label upholstered furniture will have on it somewhere.

W *means safe to clean with water*
S *means use dry cleaning solvent only*
WS *means you can use either*
X *means keep water away—vacuum or brush only*

(If there's no label, test the solution you'd like to use in an inconspicuous spot.)

Vinyl upholstery. Damp-wipe with all-purpose cleaner solution and buff dry. Treat with vinyl conditioner occa-sionally. Never use anything oily or abrasive, or any solvent on it.

Glass/metal Just use your spray bottle of glass cleaner and a cleaning cloth to polish dry.

For how to shampoo upholstered furniture, and for other furniture not covered here i.e. wicker, leather, plush, plastic, etc. see *The Cleaning Encyclopedia* and *How Do I Clean the Moosehead!*

Appliances

Get heavy use—which means a lot of drips, spills, overflows, and smudges. The first rule of appliance care is **CLEAN IT NOW**—when it happens. Now it's easy, if you wait it'll be tough and time-consuming.

Rule #2: Don't do anything that might damage the slick, smooth, dirt and stain resistant surface of your appliances.

Enamel and porcelain are strong but they can't withstand scouring cleansers, steel wool, colored nylon scrub pads, etc. These will only leave you with a scratched, dull surface that's hard to clean forever after.

Refrigerator

As needed—which will be often—spray and wipe the exterior with glass cleaner and wipe out the shelves quickly with clean dishwater. An occasional coat of appliance or car wax (keep it off plastic or rubber parts) will give the exterior a little extra shine and protection and help prevent sweating.

A couple of times a year unplug the fridge and vacuum the coils or fins or whatever there is behind there. It'll save energy and keep things safer, too.

When you finally face up to cleaning out the inside, use liquid dishwashing detergent or all-purpose cleaner or any MILD cleaner. A solution of 3 tablespoons of baking soda to a quart of water will deodorize as it cleans. Wet down any stubborn spots you come to and give them a chance to soften so you can just wipe them away.

Remove any removables and wash them in a sinkful of sudsy water; rinse and dry before replacing.

Remember this is where you store your FOOD so don't overlook/ignore all the drips and smears that will soon be growing mold (if they aren't already) under the drawers and shelves, in the door gasket folds, in the egg trays, the drip pan, etc.

Freezer

Wipe out the inside with the same gentle solutions described above, never scrub or scrape with anything sharp. If you have to defrost first you can speed the process with pots or pans full of hot water, or a portable fan pointed inside.

Range

If you have one of the newer blessedly smooth and uncomplicated ceramic cooktops, consult your owner's manual. These don't have all the ridges and niches to collect grease and spills the old type had, but you do have to be careful how you clean them. GENTLY, and only with a perfectly clean paper towel or cloth, is the general word.

As for the conventional type range, all good dishwashers know that you wipe the top (including the burner rings) and front (knobs, too) every day as you finish up the dishes. Hit the front with glass cleaner when you're doing an overall kitchen cleaning.

If you're up against accumulated grease and hardened spills, use heavy-duty cleaner or degreaser solution and a white nylon scrub sponge. If that doesn't do it you can move to a plastic or stainless steel Chore Boy type scrubber, but be sure to keep it good and wet when you work with it. You might want to soak the burner pans or drip pan overnight in degreaser—whenever you can, here, soak rather than scrub. For really tough cases it may help to soak,

then pull out the article in question and scrub away any already-softened stuff, then soak again.

The area under the rangetop usually collects enough stray spaghetti and petrified peas, etc. that you might want to whisk or vacuum it out first. Then apply degreaser solution, let it soak a while, scrub if necessary, and repeat until clean.

Self-Cleaning Ovens

The cleaning cycle of these turns any splatters, etc., left inside to ash that can just be wiped away, so there are only a couple things I need to remind you of here. One is to never use oven cleaner on any part of a self-cleaning oven, and the other is to always clean the area outside the gasket BEFORE you turn on the cleaning cycle. Otherwise the intense heat of the cycle will bake any spills, stains, or smudges on so hard you may never get them off without damaging the surface. (Check your owner's manual for any other special instructions for your model.)

Conventional Ovens

Mean using oven cleaner, usually lye, which is very mean stuff. So put an old blanket or dropcloth down around the oven (this will protect the floor better than papers). Protect yourself with rubber gloves and long sleeves, and don't breathe in when you're spraying.

Wrap aluminum foil around the light bulb and heating element to protect them, too, and apply a good thick coat of cleaner to everything else. Then WAIT a good long time—preferably overnight—to give the cleaner a chance to dissolve the grease. Then wipe off all you can of the resulting brown sludge with paper towels, or even a spatula or small squeegee.

Reapply cleaner to any remaining grease and again give it time to work. Don't scrub, just keep recoating and waiting as necessary and you should be able to wipe away every last trace.

Last, rinse well with a damp cloth (wiping with a vinegar/water solution first will neutralize the remaining cleaner and make rinsing easier).

P.S. The easy way to clean oven racks is to lay them on newspaper outside and coat both sides well with oven cleaner, then seal them up in a plastic bag somewhere safe from kids and pets. The next day you should be able to just rinse them clean and shiny.

Range hoods

Are usually coated with fuzzy grease which not only looks bad but can be a fire hazard. Consult your owner's manual for the details of cleaning your particular model, but in general you go about it as follows: Remove the motor and fan, if removable, to give yourself a little more room to maneuver.

Remove the grill, the filter, and the lens diffuser of the light if any, and soak them in hot degreaser solution until they come clean. You can also run the filter through the dishwasher by itself. Replace the charcoal filter if your hood has one.

Then wipe the worst of the grease off the hood itself with paper towels or a plastic scraper and wash the hood inside and out with degreaser. Use a white nylon scrub sponge as necessary. Wipe off the fan blades and motor housing, too, but never immerse the motor or spray anything on it.

After everything is good and dry, reassemble.

> For more detail on care of every kind of appliance, see *The Cleaning Encyclopedia.*

3 $\frac{1}{2}$ Minute Bathroom

Yes, less than five minutes a day is what it'll take you, if you clean your bathrooms the way the professionals do, with a quick daily cleaning rather than a grit-your-teeth weekly scrubbing siege. The pro approach doesn't just save time and make bathroom cleaning less depressing. It prevents the biggest problem of bathroom cleanup, which isn't mere dirt but the hard-to-remove accumulation of hard water scale and soap scum.

With the pro approach you'll no longer be attacking your bathroom fixtures with heavy artillery like abrasive cleaners and harsh scrub pads, which scratch and damage plastic, Formica, fiberglass, chrome, and porcelain, making them collect dirt faster and much harder to clean.

What do you use?

Disinfectant cleaner (see p. 16) in a spray bottle, plus a terry cleaning cloth, and white nylon backed scrub sponge, and a bowl swab. The disinfectant cleaner sanitizes as it cleans, which means it kills the germs that **cause** odors. So you won't need any more perfumes or air fresheners for the "powder room" either.

The 3 1/2 Minute Routine

Spray and wipe the mirror with glass cleaner, and whisk any hair or whiskers out of the sink with a piece of damp toilet paper. Now do the sink itself, the counter/vanity top, and the sink hardware, using your bottle of disinfectant cleaner to give things a light spray, then polishing them dry with the cleaning cloth. If you hit a bit of stubborn soil, use the nylon side of the scrub sponge on it. Spray a little ahead of yourself, so the cleaner has a few seconds to dissolve the soil.

Move to the tub and shower walls, and do them the same way.

When you reach the toilet, squirt some cleaner on your swab and swish it round the bowl. Then spray and buff the outside of the toilet (which is usually dirtier than the inside), working from top to bottom. Then wipe up around the bowl and the rest of the floor with your cleaning cloth, which is by now damp with disinfectant cleaner.

If you already have a buildup problem

Here's what to use on it (all available at a janitorial-supply store):

Hard water scale: professional strength phosphoric acid cleaner.
Soap scum: degreaser or soap scum remover.
Toilet bowl buildup: bowl cleaner (usually phosphoric or hydrochloric acid)—handle with care!

How to beat bowl buildup

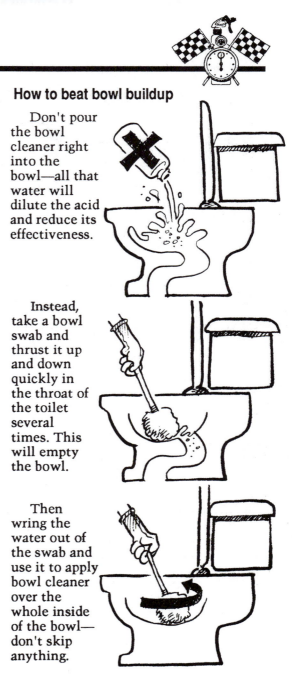

Don't pour the bowl cleaner right into the bowl—all that water will dilute the acid and reduce its effectiveness.

Instead, take a bowl swab and thrust it up and down quickly in the throat of the toilet several times. This will empty the bowl.

Then wring the water out of the swab and use it to apply bowl cleaner over the whole inside of the bowl—don't skip anything.

Leave the acid on a few minutes and flush to rinse. Reapply if necessary. Persistent rings can be removed with a WET pumice stone.

A short lesson in
Floor Care

The dirt and grit on floors is always being tromped and ground in, so all hard floors will last and look good longer if they're cleaned regularly. Most hard floors will benefit from a protective coating of some kind, for the same reason.

The floor, more than any other part of the house, projects the overall image of your home.

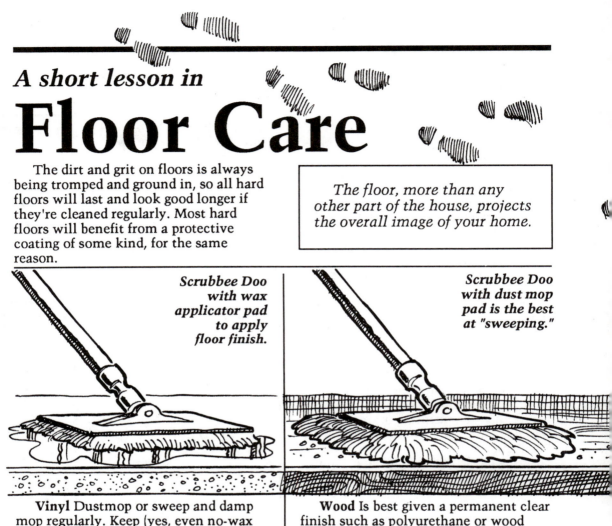

Scrubbee Doo with wax applicator pad to apply floor finish.

Scrubbee Doo with dust mop pad is the best at "sweeping."

Vinyl Dustmop or sweep and damp mop regularly. Keep (yes, even no-wax vinyl) coated with floor finish or "wax" to make it easier to clean and prevent dulling and damage. When rewaxing, do traffic areas only to prevent wax buildup.

Wood Is best given a permanent clear finish such as polyurethane or wood sealer to protect it from water and stains. Then dustmop and damp-mop regularly—apply the solution sparingly and remove it quickly when you're mopping. You can also wax sealed wood to give it further shine and protection, especially if it's gotten a little worn and dull.

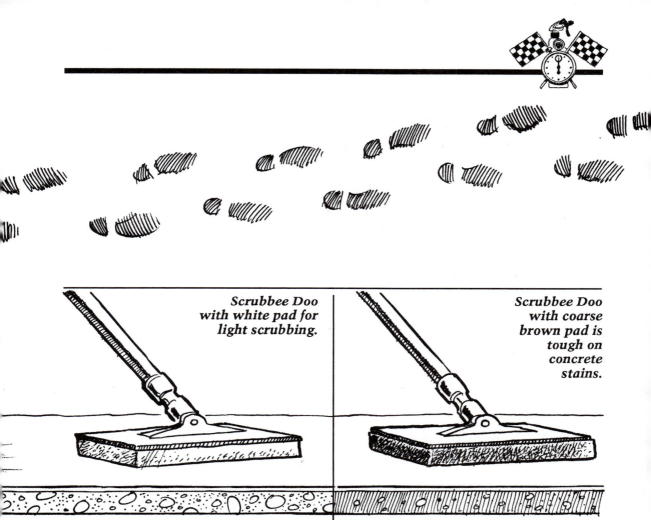

Scrubbee Doo with white pad for light scrubbing.

Scrubbee Doo with coarse brown pad is tough on concrete stains.

Tile (Stone, brick, ceramic, clay, quarry, etc.) There are hundreds of types and styles, so it's hard to generalize here. Do remember why you chose the type you did—don't constantly be trying to transform it into something else. The matte or "rustic" type isn't going to have a mirror finish no matter what you do, for example. Don't wax the shiny type— the surface is so slippery wax won't stick to it. Detergent residue is what causes dullness and streaking on shiny tile—don't use too much cleaner when you mop and use a little white vinegar in your rinse water to eliminate it. Seal the grout on all tile so dirt and stains won't have anywhere to lodge.

Concrete Will not only absorb stains like mad, but shed gritty dust constantly if it's left raw. Let concrete floors cure for at least a month if they're newly laid and clean them well with heavy-duty cleaner if they've been down a while. Then seal them with concrete seal. They'll look better, stay cleaner, and be a cinch to dustmop or damp mop thereafter.

For more on cleaning and caring for any type of hard floor, see *The Cleaning Encyclopedia* and *Is There Life After Housework!*

Dust Mopping

You do want to get the loose dirt off your hard floors before it has a chance to be ground into the finish. But sweeping it up with a broom isn't the best way. Brooms are fine for quick cleanups of small areas, but if it's a hard smooth floor or any size, a dust mop will do it better and faster. A dust mop will cover more ground in less time, it's less tiring to use, and it doesn't stir or fling dust up into the air. So go to a janitorial-supply store and get yourself a pro-quality dustmop with an 18" head and a swivel handle. While you're there get some "dust treatment" too.

How to Dust Mop

1 First you need to treat the mop head with the dust treat so it will be able to pick up and hold even the finest dust and dirt. Apply it according to directions, being sure to use the right amount—not too much or too little—for the size mop you have. And give the treatment time to really soak into the mop before you use it. Apply it and then wrap the head up in a plastic bag overnight. Once the mop is in use you'll have to add a little more treat from time to time, to keep it at full pickup power.

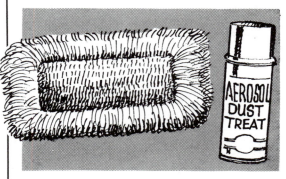

2 Mop with a smooth steady motion, always keeping the same edge of the mop forward (the swivel action will help you do this when you change direction). And never lift the mop head off the floor. If you follow these two rules you won't lose any of the dirt.

3 The pros like to mop with a side to side "S" movement, but you can also mop in a straight line. If you mop in straight lines shake off the dust load at the end of each pass, and then mop all your little piles up together at the end.

4 Shake or vacuum out the head when it gets loaded up, and wash it when it gets really dirty. Don't forget to re-treat after laundering.

5 Hang your dust mop to store it, don't lean it against the wall or floor or it'll leave an oily spot.

Broom Basics

When you do need to sweep, forget about the old corn broom. Get yourself an angle broom. These suit our natural sweeping stroke better (when you use it the whole head—not just part of it—is in contact with the floor).

They also reach into corners and tight spots better, and the flagged-tip bristles can catch even the finest dirt. These brooms also shed less and because the bristles are plastic you don't have to worry about them getting wet, unlike a corn broom.

Get a professional-strength angle broom from a janitorial-supply store and hang it up when it's not in use or the bristles will get a permanent wave.

When you sweep, drag the tips of the bristles across the floor, don't flick the broom head around or you'll kick dirt up into the air. Get the edges and corners of the room first and then the middle.

When it's time to pick up your dirt piles, a dust pan with a flexible lip (or a molded all-plastic pan) will give you the best chance of getting up every last bit.

For rough surfaces like sidewalks and driveways and unsealed concrete anywhere, a push broom is best. Get one with a 24-inch head, a handle brace, and plastic or nylon bristles. The type with a ring of finer bristles around the outside is good if you have to deal with fine dust here, too.

Damp Mopping

To remove the soil from foot traffic, spills, and airborne grease that accumulates on hard floors and makes them dull and sticky. Do it regularly and save big scrubbing and stripping jobs later.

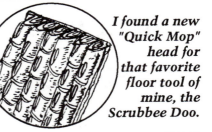

I found a new "Quick Mop" head for that favorite floor tool of mine, the Scrubbee Doo.

Choose your tools:

OR   OR

For small areas, just right for mostly carpeted homes:
- Sponge mop, professional strength with built-in wringer handle
- Bucket with cleaning solution (not more than half full to prevent splashes)
- Empty bucket

For large areas and homes with acres of hard floor:
- String mop (12 oz.)
- Bucket with cleaner
- Wringer bucket
(I like the roller wringer type) You never want to wring a string mop with your bare hands, it picks up pins, glass, etc. that hide in the strings.

For every home:
- Scrubbee Doo with scrubbing pads and Quick Mop pad
- Bucket with cleaner
- Empty bucket

A Quick Mop is wrung by hand, so look before you squeeze.

Mopping means going over the floor twice—once to soften the soil and once to remove it.

How to damp mop

1 Sweep, dustmop, or vacuum the floor first. Otherwise you'll just be making dirt soup.

2 Prepare your solution. Plain water won't do it, you need a cleaner to remove soil. Vinegar won't do it either—it may squeak, but it's not a cleaner. Use neutral all-purpose cleaner or ordinary liquid dishwashing detergent but don't use too much, be sure to follow label directions for dilution. More doesn't do better, it just causes problems, cuts the wax and dulls the floor finish.

3 Spread the solution generously over an area within arm's reach—5 or 6 square feet (don't flood it, though). Then leave it on there at least a minute or two to dissolve the dirt. Cover a manageable area, so it won't dry before you get back to it.

4 If you come across some stubborn soil, scrub a bit with your mop. If it's something tougher like a black mark or a hardened jam blob, go after it with a green nylon pad.

5 Now wring the mop as dry as possible and go over the whole floor again to pick up the sludge. Rinse and wring the mop once or twice as you go if the floor is really dirty.

Repeat until your whole floor is clean.

When you mop, it's a good idea to mop all around the edge of the room first ("frame the floor") and then do all the rest with figure 8 strokes, staying well away from the edges. This will prevent the slopped-up baseboards mopping often means.

More Scrubbee Doo help:

Scrub pads for every job!

Swivel action head has gripper teeth underneath to grab and hold pads, yet peel off easily.

White: light duty cleaning, bathroom tile, glass, etc.; Blue: no-wax floor, tile, walls, etc.; Brown: heavy-duty stripping, concrete floors, etc.

Quick Mop soaks it all up. And the Wax Applicator pad makes finish smooth and shiny!

Stripping

Or removing all the wax right down to the bare floor.

When the whole floor is dark and dirty looking, even after mopping, and the edges have a buildup of discolored old wax, it's time to strip!

How To Strip a Floor

1 Sweep or vacuum it well first and then mix up a solution of professional wax stripper from a janitorial-supply store (if you tell them what type of flooring you have they'll fix you up with exactly the right kind). Mop the solution out onto about a 10 x 10' area of the floor and leave it. Apply more solution if it starts to dry.

2 By now the wax should be softening and dissolving, but if you have a bad case of buildup, you may still need to do some scrubbing. Put a brown or black nylon stripping pad on a long-handled floor scrubber (Scrubbee Doo) or a single-disc floor polisher, if it's a large floor, and go over the floor twice. The first time will help the stripper finish penetrating the wax, and the second time should loosen and remove it. Re-wet the floor as necessary during this operation, to keep it from drying out.

3 Check for unremoved wax by running your fingernail or the edge of a coin across the floor, or simply look around for any remaining dark patches. If you find still more coming up, add more solution and scrub more as necessary.

4 Squeegee all the sludge into a puddle with a floor squeegee and scoop it up with a dustpan. You can also use a wet/dry vac to vacuum it up. Either way, it's much faster than using a mop.

5 Now you have to be sure to remove any residue from the stripper or the new wax won't bond to the floor as it should. If you're using a "rinseless" wax remover, one rinse is enough. Otherwise mop-rinse the floor twice and add a cup of white vinegar per gallon of water to the first rinse.

6 Let the floor dry well and you're ready to rewax.

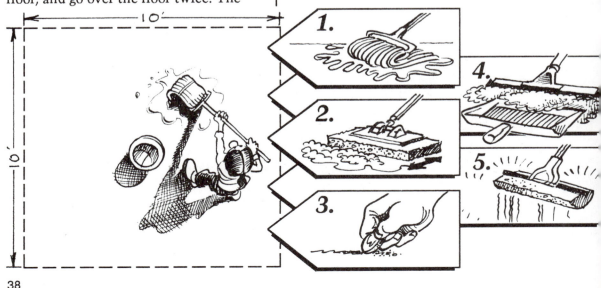

1.

2.

3.

4.

5.

Waxing

Doesn't just make floors shinier and better looking. It protects your floors from abrasion (from soil and grit and foot traffic) and lengthens their life. It also makes them easier to sweep and clean and when you get black marks on the floor they're a snap to remove because they're on the surface of the wax, not the floor itself. Even No-Wax floors need waxing to keep them from eventually becoming worn damaged and dull.

What's the best wax to use?

Modern floor dressings are technically called "floor finishes," but most of us still call them "wax." The kind you want is a commercial metal interlock or polymer self-polishing such as Top Gloss.

When you wax, several thin coats are always better than one thick sloppy one.

How to Wax a Floor

1 First make sure the floor is good and clean and free from detergent or stripper residue. If in doubt, give it a neutralizing rinse of water plus 1/2 cup white vinegar per gallon.

2 You want something to apply your wax that is not only clean, but used only for this. And that will enable you to spread it in a nice thin even film, without bubbling or foaming. Ideally this would be a lambswool applicator head on a long-handled floor scrubber, but it could also be a sponge mop or a small mop or a clean cloth folded into a pad. Wet it first and wring it as dry as possible.

3 Pour out some wax into a little puddle on the floor and spread it with your applicator, using smooth even strokes. It's a good idea to overlap your strokes to get good coverage and avoid skips, but don't go over any area more than 3 times. If you go over and over it, or go back over the surface after it's partly dry, you'll have a streaky mess.

4 Keep pouring out little puddles and spreading them till the whole floor is covered with one thin coat. Then let it dry well.

5 If you're waxing a newly stripped floor, you'll want to apply 2 more thin coats **to the traffic areas only**, being sure to let one coat dry well before applying the next.

6 Don't forget to rinse your applicator out well when you're done, or it'll be stiff as a board the next time you need it.

If your floor is so old and dull and worn that waxing won't do a thing for it, you may want to apply a sealer to it first (see p. 8). After that, waxing should bring back some life and shine.

For more waxing wisdom, see *The Cleaning Encyclopedia* and *How Do I Clean The Moosehead!*

Basic Carpet Care

Carpet is wonderful in that a whisk over the surface with a carpet sweeper or vacuum will keep it presentable for quite a while.

But if you want your "soft floors" to last as long as they should, and look "company good" the whole time, they need more than that. Like everything else we own, they need some basic preventive maintenance.

The reason is simple. The dirt and grit that's tracked into our homes doesn't just lay there on the surface. It gets tromped into the carpet, and soon it's soiling and grinding and wearing away at the carpet fibers from the roots, the bottom, of the carpet as well as the top. A good carpet maintenance program means regularly removing not only the obvious but the embedded soil.

How do you do that?

1 Install walkoff mats to reduce the amount of soil brought in (see p. 6).

2 Remove spots and spills (see p. 45) on carpeting immediately (and check out a copy of my *Stainbuster's Bible* for how to remove specific spots).

3 VACUUM regularly with a vac capable of getting out embedded soil

before it damages the carpet. This means a vacuum with a beater brush, brush roll, or beater bar. The traffic patterns get the most tracked into them, so you want to do them several times a week. The whole carpet should be done about weekly, though you can let the edges and under and behind things go longer.

4 Surface clean your carpet (see p. 43) about once a month to give it a "face lift" and prevent "cow trails" (dark ugly paths) from developing.

5 Deep clean or "shampoo" your carpet when it needs it—once every couple years is enough for most carpet. This will clean it all the way down to the roots.

> **For more on any aspect of carpet care, see *The Cleaning Encyclopedia* or *Is There Life After Housework!.***

Professional Secrets of Better Vacuuming

Concentrate on the traffic areas or the "cow trails." This is where most of the dirt is, and where soil and grit are going to be ground in under foot to ugly up and damage your carpet.

Likewise, **don't sweat the edges**, or worry about moving the furniture to get under and behind things every time you vacuum. You might find a bit of dust or a dropped sock or magazine in places like these, but what little dirt there is doesn't get tromped in. So you don't need to do edges, especially, more than twice a month or so and you can let them go longer than that as long as they don't LOOK bad.

Police first—it's a vacuum, not a garbage disposal. So before you start, be sure to pick up all the "big stuff" that is only going to clog or injure your vacuum—all those toy trucks, big pebbles and dirt clods, crumpled tissues, peanut shells, nuts and bolts, broken crayons, dropped quarters...

Hold the vacuum cord in your free hand, or drape it over your shoulder, and **vacuum into the room, instead of out**—and you won't be fighting the cord every inch of the way.

Slow down—it's faster in the long run. One leisurely stroke will beat three

41

short swipes any day. Take your time, and let your vacuum do the work. Give the beater bar a chance to loosen the dirt and the suction a chance to pick it up.

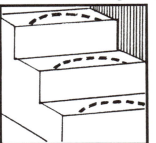

Stairs only need beater-bar action (to get out embedded dirt) on the center of the tread, and you can lift your upright vacuum up on there to do that. The corners and that dust-accumulating area where the steps and risers meet can just be wiped clean with a damp cloth.

Don't ignore that little feature/knob called "pile adjustment." If it's set too high the beater bar won't be able to reach the carpet to vibrate the dirt out; if it's too low it'll interfere with both beater bar action and air flow (suction!). You want it set so that the beater bar just comes in light contact with the carpet.

Use the air bleeder on your canister vacuum's hose when you're vacuuming things like drapes. It'll reduce the suction just enough so your vacuum can pick up the dust without swallowing the curtain.

"...and what vacuum do I use?

EUREKA!

TLC for your most important piece of household machinery—your Vacuum

To keep your faithful servant running long and strong:

Keep the bag emptied Don't wait till it's crammed full. Anything above half full begins to cut your vacuum's suction.

Don't run over the cord or close doors over it, etc. And remove the plug from the outlet with your hand, not by a yank from across the room.

Don't let string, thread, hair, etc. accumulate on the beater brush or bar.

It'll reduce your vacuum's pickup power, and it's hard on the bearings, too. Work the point of a pair of scissors under all this and snip away until the brush spins freely again.

Check the brushes on the beater brush—and if they're mashed and worn, replace them. It's easy to do.

If you seem to be losing suction, have a repair person **check the fan or impeller**, the part that creates the air flow we call suction. If the blades are chipped or worn, replace it (it doesn't cost much). You'll think you got a new vac.

Introduction to Surface Cleaning

The professionals' secret for keeping carpet looking crisp and new, preventing "cow trails" (ugly, discolored dirt paths), and delaying the need for deep cleaning. It's sort of a quick shampooing of the surface of the rug.

The most practical ways to do it at home:

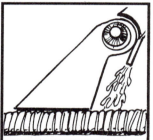

Do-it-yourself Extraction

With one of the machines now made by companies like Bissell and Sears for do-it-yourself home extraction cleaning of carpet. Machines like these don't really have strong enough injection pressure or suction, or get the solution hot enough for all-the-way-down-to-the-roots shampooing, but they're perfect for surface cleaning.

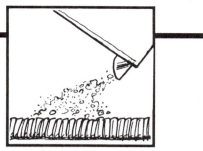

Powder Dry Cleaning

With one of the carpet-cleaning powders made by Host, Capture, Amway and Sears, among others. You scrub them in by hand or machine and then vacuum them back out.

Bonnet Cleaning

For the "Bonnet" method you dampen a yarn pad or disc called a bonnet with a special solvent cleaning solution and rub it into the carpet, with a floor buffer, a moplike tool, or even by hand.

For complete surface cleaning instructions see *The Cleaning Encyclopedia* and *Is There Life After Housework!*.

The Pro Lowdown on Carpet Shampooing

Or the deep cleaning we have to do every so often to remove the dirt and soil down deep in the pile.

The following are the most common methods and their pros and cons:

Hot Water Extraction or "steam" cleaning. A hot cleaning solution is shot into the carpet and then a strong wet/dry vac pulls it back out. Extraction will usually remove loose soil even from deep in the carpet but it doesn't do so well with embedded soil. That's because the solution isn't on the carpet long enough to have a chance to break down stubborn dirt and there's no "agitation" or scrubbing action to help get it out. If you use this method you want to be sure the carpet is presprayed or prespotted and that the solution is hot enough (150°f) to do a good job—this usually calls for professional truck-mounted equipment.

Rotary Shampooing Carpet shampoo is scrubbed in with a floor polisher or buffer and then removed with a wet/dry vac, or left to dry and then picked up with a regular vacuum. Rotary cleaning does an excellent job of loosening embedded soil, but may not then actually remove it all. This method also usually leaves shampoo residue behind that accelerates resoiling.

Dry Cleaning is done with a powder containing solvents and detergents which is worked into the carpet by hand or machine and then vacuumed up.

There's no water involved and no long waits for the carpet to dry. But this method is also slow and expensive and it's not easy to get all the powder back out.

The Best Method is a combination of rotary cleaning and hot water extraction, which gives you the best of both worlds. The whole carpet, or at least the badly soiled parts and the traffic paths, is scrubbed with a buffer, and then rinsed with an extractor. This kind of "showcase" cleaning can also be accomplished by an extractor that has agitator heads.

Should you do it yourself?

There's a lot of reasons not to. The average homemaker doesn't have access to equipment capable of doing a really good job, and is all too likely to end up with an overwet carpet, too much shampoo residue, stains that are still there, and a strained back and scratched car upholstery from hauling rental equipment around. The odds of a disappointing job of cleaning and damage to household furnishings are good. And if you counted the value of your time and the aggravation of it all, it's probably more expensive than having it professionally done.

If you do hire it done get and check references on the company you have in mind, and get a firm price before they start.

For more about carpet shampooing including how to go about it if you do it yourself, see *Is There Life After Housework!* and *The Cleaning Encyclopedia*.

Spot Removal

Your Own Spot Removal Kit

Keep on hand to attack fresh spills: Clean white terry cloths (white absorbent cloth so you can check for colorfastness and see if the stain is coming out or not). A spotting brush (available at janitorial-supply stores) and scraper (a dull butter knife will serve the purpose). Neutral detergent such as liquid dishwashing detergent (dilute 20:1 for spotting). Clear household ammonia (don't use on silk or wool). White vinegar (dilute 1:1 with water for cotton, linen, and acetate). Dry spotter or dry-cleaning fluid such as Energine, Carbona, or Afta.

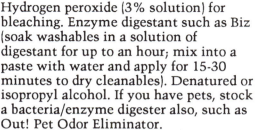

Hydrogen peroxide (3% solution) for bleaching. Enzyme digestant such as Biz (soak washables in a solution of digestant for up to an hour; mix into a paste with water and apply for 15-30 minutes to dry cleanables). Denatured or isopropyl alcohol. If you have pets, stock a bacteria/enzyme digester also, such as Out! Pet Odor Eliminator.

What does it mean when it says...

Pretreat: apply pretreat or a paste of laundry detergent on the stain for 15-30 minutes prior to washing to loosen the stain so the washer can flush it away.

Sponge: lay the stain face down on a pad of clean white absorbent cloth and use another such pad, dampened with spotter, to push the spotter through the stained fabric into the pad below.

Feather: Rinse and dry a spot from the outside in, to blend in the edges and avoid leaving a ring.

1. Catch it while it's fresh; chances for removal are 75% better. Don't iron or hot-air dry until the stain is gone—heat sets most stains.

2. First blot up all the liquid and scrape up all the solids you can. On a large liquid spill you can use a wet/dry vacuum. Be careful not to spread the stain.

3. Test any chemical you intend to use in a hidden area to make sure it won't discolor or damage the surface.

4. Apply spotter, and work from the outside of the stain in, to avoid spreading. Blot, don't scrub; strike with the flat face of a spotting brush if needed to help break up the stain.

5. Rinse chemical spotters out with water, blot dry and feather the edges. Brush or fluff up pile or nap.

6. On carpet and upholstery, put a thick pad of toweling over the spot, weight it down with books, and leave it there for several hours to "wick up" any remaining moisture.

LCOHOL

Blot up all you can and sponge the spot with water. Sponge with detergent solution; blot. Sponge with vinegar; blot; rinse. Bleach with hydrogen peroxide if necessary.

LOOD

Blot or scrape up all you can; soak old blood stains in salt water or digestant. Blot with cool water. Blot with ammonia; rinse. Bleach with hydrogen peroxide if necessary. If stain remains, try rust remover from a janitorial-supply store.

ANDLE WAX

Scrape off all you can first with a scraper or butter knife. Put a clean absorbent cloth over the spot and iron with a warm iron to melt and absorb the wax into the blotting cloth. Remove remaining residue with dry-cleaning fluid.

HOCOLATE

Scrape off all you can first. Sponge with dry-cleaning fluid. Sponge with detergent solution; blot; rinse. If stain remains, bleach with hydrogen peroxide.

IGARETTE BURNS

For slight discoloration, rub with dry steel wool, vacuum up the debris, then apply detergent solution. Trim off blackened tufts with scissors. For bad burns, have a repairperson "doughnut cut" the damaged area out and plug a new piece in.

OFFEE

Blot with detergent solution; rinse. Blot with vinegar; rinse; air-dry. If stain remains, sponge with dry-cleaning fluid. Bleach any remaining stain with hydrogen peroxide.

RASS

Sponge with water. Sponge with alcohol (except wool, silk, or acetate). If stain remains, use digestant, then sponge with detergent solution; rinse. Bleach with hydrogen peroxide if necessary.

REASY FOODS

Gently scrape off all you can. Sponge with dry-cleaning fluid. Sponge with detergent solution. If stain remains, use digestant, then sponge with detergent solution; rinse. Bleach any remaining stain with hydrogen peroxide.

GUM

Use aerosol gum freeze from a janitorial-supply store or dry ice to harden the gum and make it brittle. Strike and break into pieces, scrape them up with a dull butter knife. Remove residue with dry-cleaning fluid.

ICE CREAM/ MILK/CREAM

Sponge with detergent solution, then with ammonia; rinse and air dry. Sponge any remaining stain with dry-cleaning fluid. If stain remains, use digestant, then sponge with detergent solution and rinse.

INK (BALLPOINT)

Sponge with detergent solution; rinse. If stain remains, saturate with cheap hair spray and blot. If still there, try alcohol, acetone, or non-oily nail polish remover and a bleach safe for the fabric, in that order. If yellow stain remains, try rust remover.

MILDEW

Dry-brush to remove as much as possible. Sponge with disinfectant solution; blot. Sponge with ammonia; rinse. Bleach with chlorine bleach if safe for fabric; if not, use hydrogen peroxide.

MUSTARD

Scrape and blot to remove all you can. Sponge with detergent solution, then with vinegar; rinse. If stain remains, bleach with hydrogen peroxide.

NAIL POLISH

Blot acetone or non-oily nail polish remover through the stain into a clean absorbent pad, test first. No acetone on acetate, modacrylic, silk, or wool, use amyl acetate (banana oil), from a pharmacy. Flush with dry-cleaning fluid; air dry. If stain remains, try alcohol, then hydrogen peroxide.

OIL

Absorb fresh oil with cornmeal, (kitty litter, or sawdust on concrete) then blot with paint thinner or dry-cleaning fluid. Feather edges. If stain remains, sponge with detergent solution; rinse and feather.

PAINT

If fresh, flush with either mineral spirits for oil-base paint or detergent solution for latex. If dry, carefully soften with lacquer thinner or paint stripper (test first for fabric damage) then flush with appropriate solvent.

47

PET STAINS

Scrape up all the solid matter you can and blot out all liquid possible by placing a clean towel on the spot and standing on it. Apply bacteria/enzyme digester according to directions. When dry, remove any remaining stain with detergent solution; rinse.

RUST

Use commercial rust remover carefully observing all safety precautions. Home remedies like salt and lemon juice are slow and not always effective.

PASTE SHOE POLISH/ LIPSTICK

Gently scrape off all you can, being extra careful not to spread the stain. Blot dry-cleaning fluid through the stain into a clean absorbent pad. Sponge with detergent solution; blot. Sponge with ammonia; rinse. If stain remains, try alcohol, then hydrogen peroxide.

SOFT DRINKS

Blot up all you can. Blot with detergent solution; rinse; air dry. If stain remains, soak with glycerin for 30 minutes and rinse.

TAR/GREASE

Scrape up all you can, then remove residue by blotting with paint thinner or dry-cleaning fluid. Blot with detergent solution; rinse.

VOMIT

Scrape up as much as possible, then rinse the spot with water. Blot with detergent solution. Blot with ammonia; rinse. If stain remains, use digestant, then sponge with detergent solution; rinse.

If you don't know what it is...

If it's a **mystery stain? Look, smell, feel,** and **ask** who did it. Next try a dry (solvent) spotter such as dry-cleaning fluid. Then if it remains use water-based spot remover.

There is **no one miracle** stain remover, most stains require a combination of chemicals and a several-stage attack.

For answers to all your spot and stain questions and problems, and even how to *prevent* stains, see *Don Aslett's Stainbuster's Bible.*

Safe
High Altitude
Cleaning

A lot of us don't like heights. We'll never look over the very edge of the Grand Canyon, we don't even like driving over a high bridge. But there they are: The flyspecks on the ceiling, the burned-out bulb in the stairwell, the cobwebs in that high corner, the grease buildup on the soffit.

Many household cleaning and repair jobs that only take five minutes to do take a half hour or more just to figure out a way to reach the area. (And too often what we rig up to do it isn't safe.)

You don't need to be buffaloed by hard-to-reach areas any longer. You only need a few pieces of the right equipment and a little know-how to reach those high places safely. No more risking life and limb standing on chairs, teetering on benches, or perching on sinks.

What tools do you need?

1 **An Extension Handle.** Many, if not most, of the operations we're always climbing to do can be done safely and efficiently right from the ground. Extension handles can be attached to lambswool dusters, squeegees, and paint rollers to extend your reach from 4 to 12 feet. Extension handles are made of aluminum or fiberglass so they're light and easy to maneuver, and they telescope down for easy storage.

49

2 **A sturdy 5-foot stepladder.** This is exactly the right size to enable you to do most indoor household jobs safely and efficiently. A 6' ladder is too tall—you'll skin up the house carrying it around, and a 4' ladder is too short—you'll be tempted to stand on the top step. Get a good strong professional-grade aluminum model and you'll have an excellent all-around helper that will last forever.

3 **A box that won't let you down.** I learned about this working for the Bell System and it's a terrific way to reach the lower heights safely: a sturdy wooden box you can make up yourself easily and inexpensively. You just set it on its side or on end and step up on it and work right from it—at last without having to worry about your "stool" giving way or sliding away. You can cut hand holes in the side to make it easy to transport from place to place, and give it a nickname or some custom decoration. You can also use a box together with ladders and a plank (see below) to do higher jobs safely.

4 **A plank 2"x12"x8'.** Yes, a plain old plank, stretched between two ladders or a ladder and your cleaning box, will give you a safe platform from which you can reach a large area to clean or paint etc. without all that climbing up and down.

5 **An extension ladder.** For those extra-high outdoor reaches—16 or 18 feet long is enough for home use and fiber-glass or wood is safer than aluminum if you have to work around electrical lines much. Always make sure the legs are seated securely, and angle the ladder one foot away from the wall for every four feet of height.

How to Wash Walls

My famous two-bucket method (introduced on p. 24) works well on any painted wall or ceiling or on vinyl wall covering or well sealed paneling. It'll give you quick streak-free results with no scrubbing! **Equipment needed:**

cellulose sponge
cleaning cloth
1 empty bucket
1 bucket 1/2 full of warm water

Cleaner to put in the water:
neutral all-purpose cleaner

OR for really dirty, greasy, smoke-stained walls, heavy-duty cleaner or degreaser. If it's paneling you'll be cleaning, oil soap is what you want to use.

How to go about it

1 Move any furniture out of the way, or if water wouldn't do an object any good and it can't be moved, put a drop-cloth or plastic sheet over it. There's very little dripping in the pro approach you're about to learn, but why take a chance.

2 Put your ladder or ladder, plank, and box assembly (opposite) into place and set your buckets as close to you as possible—on the floor right up against the wall is best. Many a cleaner has started on the walls and ended up spending all his time mopping up the floor!

3 Dip your sponge into the bucket of cleaner just about 1/2 inch, so you get enough solution to wet the wall but not enough to splash and run all over.

4 Start at the top of the wall and spread the solution in an area you can reach easily (about 3-foot by 3-foot is right for most of us). Go easy, don't press on the sponge or solution will run out and down the wall.

By the time you reach the end of that 3' x 3' section, the solution will have loosened the dirt, so now you can go back over the area again lightly with your sponge to pick it all up and remove it.

Now with a folded cleaning cloth, wipe the surface and polish it dry. This will remove any dirt or solution left on there and prevent streaks. If it's enamel paint you're cleaning, to insure a streak-free surface you'll need to do a little extra buffing and change your cleaning cloth the minute it starts getting damp. If you're working on paneling, be sure to buff with the grain.

Squeeze, don't wring, the sponge over the empty bucket and then dip it 1/2 inch again into the bucket of solution and continue on. The empty bucket will gradually fill with dark, dirty water and your bucket of solution will stay clean and clear. No longer will you find yourself working with polluted cleaning solution that's lost its full power!

Spots or Black Marks

If you come across them, wash right over them, they might just come off with all the rest. If they don't, come back to them when you're done and rub them gently with a cleaning cloth moistened in the solution. (Don't start scrubbing with cleansers or abrasive pads or peanut butter or you'll remove the mark, all right, along with the surface of the paint, and be left with a dull patch more visible than the original mark.) If the cloth doesn't get it, try a white nylon scrub sponge moistened in solution—first the sponge side, then the nylon side. If all else fails you can try some dry cleaning fluid on a black mark.

When you do have to resort to "sanding" a mark off with abrasive, use as little as possible and work carefully to keep the damage as small as possible.

Woodwork

Wait till you're finished with the walls to do it, or all the hair, lint, and dead bugs that are always on there will get on your sponge and then all over the walls.

Just take a damp cleaning cloth and wipe it down the woodwork to pick up all the debris. Then if it's really dirty, you can go back over the area with a solution-dampened sponge and then a fresh dry cloth.

The Dry Sponge

The secret weapon of the professionals for cleaning porous surfaces such as flat paint, wallpaper, masonry, and acoustic tile, and things like lampshades that can't be wet-cleaned. Dry sponges are used for wood paneling, vinyl wall covering, and oil paintings, too, and they'll remove smoke or soot from almost anything. They won't take off smears, smudges, fingerprints, or greasy soil, but they'll swiftly remove the surface film of dirt.

Exactly What Is It?

A soft foam-rubber like sponge available as a 5" x 7" x 1/2" pad or a 2" x 2" x 6" block. The block is designed to be mounted on a pole for easy ceiling cleaning, but the pad gives you more useable surface, which is important, because absorbency is what a dry sponge is all about.

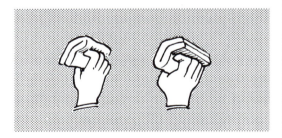

How To Use It

To use a dry sponge, fold it in half and hold it as shown and wipe it lightly across the surface, overlapping your strokes a little. When that part of the sponge gets dirty and doesn't seem to be removing the dirt as well, switch to a clean part and keep swiping. Never get a dry sponge wet and don't try to recycle it—when it's grungy all over just discard it and switch to a fresh one.

For more on dry sponges and how to use them to speed your cleaning, see *Is There Life After Housework!* and *The Cleaning Encyclopedia.*

Windows

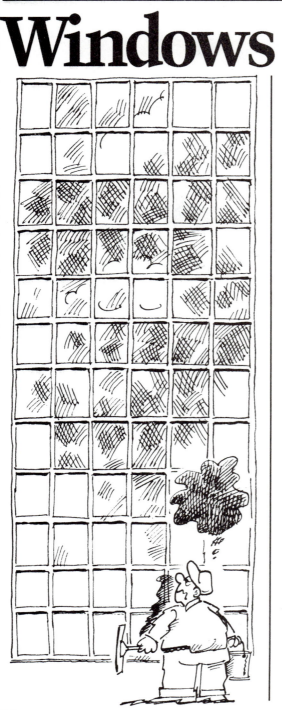

An easy job that most people dread...

You won't dread it any more if you do them like the professionals do... with a squeegee! This is the right way to do any full-size window or large expanse of glass. It's not only easier and cheaper, it gets windows cleaner and they'll stay clean longer afterward.

Equipment needed: (all of which you can find at a janitorial-supply store)
- 10 or 12" professional quality brass squeegee such as the Ettore
- window scrubber such as the Golden Glove
- extension pole if you're doing high windows
- bucket with cleaning solution (see below)

Squeegeeing in short:

Don't let the idea of it intimidate you. All you do is apply cleaning solution with the wand or sponge, and then remove it (along with all the dirt) with the squeegee.

1 Wipe around the outside edge of the window with a damp cloth to remove any debris that otherwise might get caught under your squeegee blade. If it's a really dirty outside window, give the whole thing a quick hosedown to get rid of mud, cobwebs, bird deposits, etc.

2 Mix up your solution: Not more than a capful of ammonia or a few drops of liquid dish detergent in a bucket of warm water—any more cleaner than that will only cause streaking.

3 Dip the flat side of the scrubber (or a sponge) just about 1/4 inch into the solution and wet the window lightly. Then go back over it to loosen any stubborn soil, and run your scrubber quickly around the window against the frame to pick up any dirt you may have shoved against it.

4 Before you start squeegeeing, wet the blade of the squeegee with a damp cloth, so it won't skip and jump around on the glass. Wipe the blade between strokes, too, when you're working with it.

5 Tilt the squeegee so that only about an inch of the blade rests lightly against the top of the window. Then pull it straight across the top to create a dry strip about an inch wide. This will prevent those maddening drops from running down from the top.

6 Put the squeegee blade in the dry area and pull it down to about 3 inches from the bottom of the window. Repeat until the whole window is done, being sure to overlap a little into the last stroke each time to keep water from running into the already-clean area.

7 Run the squeegee along the bottom of the window now to remove the accumulated water and wipe the sill with a dry cloth.

8 Resist the temptation to remove any lingering water drops or little marks along the frame etc. with a cloth. Just let them dry and fade away or if you must wipe, use the tip of your bare finger (by now it will be oil-free, and the perfect touchup tool!).

- Don't clean windows in direct sunlight—they'll dry too fast and streak
- With some windows, you may want to "cut the water" off the sides as well as the top, and then squeegee the rest of the window with horizontal strokes.
- Small decorative panes are best done with a spray bottle of window cleaner and a cleaning cloth or paper towel (not old newspapers!).

For more detail on the professional way of cleaning windows, see *Is There Life After Housework!* or *The Cleaning Encyclopedia.*

Blinds

We all hate to clean them, but the way to make it more bearable, believe it or not, is to do it more often!

If you dust them regularly (rather than when it can't be put off any longer) the dust won't have a chance to combine with oils and moisture in the air into a stubborn sticky coating that's almost impossible to remove.

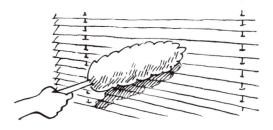

Dust them once a month or so, with a Masslinn cloth (see p. 18) or better yet, a lambswool duster. Close them up flat, dust one side, then close them the other way and dust the other. If you're using a lambswool duster, be sure to make good contact with the surface, don't just wave it over the slats.

Verticals shed dust, so they can usually be done less often. Cloth-covered verticals, however, will absorb dust, so they should be done monthly too, and not with a treated dustcloth, because they will also absorb dust treatment. Use a vacuum dust brush.

Deep Cleaning

The easy and ideal way to do this is by **ultrasonic cleaning**. You just look in the Yellow pages under Blinds—Cleaning and find a professional who specializes in this. When your blinds come back even the cords and tapes will be dazzlingly clean.

Washing

Washing is the other way to deep clean. Don't even try to do this in the bathtub or on the window.

1 Go outside, and find a flat, slightly slanted surface such as a driveway, and spread out an old quilt or blanket on it.

2 Let the blind out all the way, make sure all the louvers are flat, and lay it on the quilt or blanket.

3 Mix up an all-purpose cleaner or ammonia solution, wet the blind with it, and scrub with a soft brush in the direction of the slats. Be sure to get up under the ribbons. Then turn the blind over and do the other side.

4 Hang the blind on the clothesline or over a ladder (or have someone hold it up) and rinse it with a hose.

5 Then give it a good shake and let it dry well before you hang it back up. Dark-colored blinds need to be blotted dry to prevent water spots.

Verticles

Verticals can be washed very neatly and quickly with a device available at janitorial supply stores called a Tricket. This is a tongs-like tool with little sponges to wash, and little squeegees to dry, both sides of the slat at once.

Cloth-covered verticals can be wiped occasionally with a cloth dampened with carpet shampoo.

How to Clean Screens

To get rid of all that accumulated dust, dirt, and bird doo.

Remove them from the window and lay them out on an old quilt, blanket, or dropcloth—make sure they're perfectly flat so they don't get damaged.

Scrub them with all-purpose cleaner or any mild detergent solution and a SOFT brush (especially if it's the modern fiberglass screening). If they're extra dirty turn them over and hit the other side, too.

Rinse with a hose and then give them a rap with your hand to shake most of the water loose.

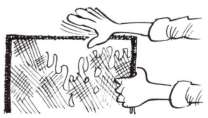

Let them sun or air-dry the rest of the way and they're done.

Pet Clean Up
Made Easy

For happy coexistence with pets you need patience and some special products (see below) not necessarily available at the supermarket—check out your local pet store or janitorial-supply store.

Cleaning up pet accidents will rarely be necessary if you take the time to housebreak your pets and pay attention to their signals, when they're sending.

If you do have to deal with a pet accident, first **clean it up right away**, don't leave it, or urine, especially, may become impossible to fully remove. Blot or scrape all you can up first, and then all you need on hard impermeable surfaces such as vinyl or laminate is simple soap and water.

Porous hard surfaces such as raw concrete and flat paint call for a chemical deodorizer cleaner such as Nilotex or Dog-Tex.

For **urine, feces, or vomit on anything absorbent** such as carpet, upholstery, or bedding, you need a bacteria/enzyme digester such as Outright Pet Odor Eliminator. Only a product like this can remove all the odor, by literally digesting the organic compounds that cause bad odors. Bacteria/enzyme digesters can be used anywhere water can be used, but you have to follow the instruction s carefully and be patient—they take up to 8 hours to work.

For **urine on carpet**, probably the #1 pet problem: blot up all you can and apply bacteria/enzyme digester. Follow up with ordinary carpet stain remover if any stain remains. Old or very extensive urine staining in carpet may be impossible to remove.

Vomit: Scrape up all you can, then flood with water to neutralize the stomach acids. Blot and apply a bacteria/enzyme digester.

Odors anywhere: Remember, you must remove the source of the odor (the dead mouse, the aged dog doo) first or you'll never get rid of the odor!

Hard floors or walls in pet areas can be cleaned with a deodorizing cleaner such as Nilodor.

When you do need to **disinfect** use a quaternary disinfectant cleaner or the disinfectant safest for pets, Chlorasan or Nolvasan. Then: Make sure all pets are out of the area when you're disinfecting; clean the area first—plain old dirt will interfere with the action of most disinfectants; protect yourself with rubber gloves or anything else the label tells you; leave the solution on at least ten minutes; and rinse well afterward.

Litter Box Logic

Plain generic litter (the cheapest!) is best and not too much of it—no more than three inches and one inch is really best. Your cats will feel more comfortable using the box and there'll be less litter kicked out. It's urine that really makes the box smell bad, so scoop out the urine "clumps" gently when you're box cleaning, not just the solid waste. Clean the box out completely once a week and wipe the area around it with disinfectant or deodorizing cleaner.

The Half-dozen best pet hair remedies

1. Groom your pet regularly—get it before it gets all over.
2. A damp cloth will whisk hair right off things like woodwork.
3. A pet rake (see p.19) is great on upholstery, drapes, car interiors, etc.
4. Wide sticky tape on or off a roller is the best clothes de-hairer.
5. A vacuum with a beater bar or brush is what you need to get it out of carpeting.
6. A dustmop does it best on hard floors.

Some handy pet cleanup helpers

A small squeegee and a dustpan make a good team for quick, neat, "hands off" removal of pet messes.

Small walkoff mats (see p. 6) are good mess catchers under the food and water dishes and by pet entrances. They make nice hair-catching pet beds, too.

A few terrible truths about fleas

They only spend about a tenth of their time on your pets—all the rest of the time they're lounging in your rugs, upholstery, and other soft surfaces. To really get rid of them, you have to treat your whole premises and all your animals at once.

Regular vacuuming will help reduce fleas, but use disposable bags and dispose of them the minute you're done.

For Pet Mess Prevention

- Confine your furry friends to less vulnerable parts of the house.
- Use tough fabrics and finishes in pet areas, and seal any susceptible porous surfaces.
- Avoid highly dyed pet foods (they can make permanent stains).
- Make sure your indoor and outdoor garbage cans have secure lids.
- Consider installing a waste digester in the backyard for dropping disposal.

For a complete guide on how to have clean, happy, healthy, sweet-smelling pets (including how to pet-proof your home and train your four-legged friends to make life easier for the both of you), see Pet Clean-Up Made Easy.

Your Own
Cleaning Business

A great way to start a second career or earn extra money. The family can even work together. Whatever your reason for considering it, the cleaning business takes very little capital to start, and is always in demand—there's always plenty of dirt around!

What tools do you need?

Basic floor and window cleaning gear (vacuum, mop, squeegee, buckets, etc.) will get you started, along with some work clothes and some roomy transportation such as an old van. You can add more as your client list and the size and number of your jobs increases.

It's a good business but not a free ride—the industry:

1. Is highly competitive (and has a high failure rate).

2. It's hard work.

3. It isn't a "prestige" position.

4. And it often involves working late or "off" hours.

BUT—Those same odd hours may be an advantage to you, your skills will always have a market, and you won't have to take fitness classes to get exercise.

To learn the business, you can:

1. Jump right in—get business cards printed up, put an ad in the paper, and go for it.
2. Work for a local cleaning contractor for a while to learn the ropes.
3. Buy an existing cleaning company or franchise (and let them train you).
4. Do some volunteer cleaning work for a while somewhere until you gain some experience and confidence cleaning for others.

Secrets of getting started

1. Do the work yourself—get some experience under your belt and some money in your pocket before you start hiring help.
2. Be especially careful about hiring good friends, relatives, and the children of clients.
3. Get and stay legal—get all the licenses, permits, insurance, etc. you need and don't dodge any tax or employment requirements.
4. Bid your jobs—don't work by the hour. You'll quickly learn how fast you are, and can bid accordingly. Bidding is the way to make big money.
5. Stick to a few basic professional chemicals—your local janitorial-supply store (and p. 16) can tell you which ones you really need.

Secrets of staying successful

1. Remember that satisfied (make that delighted!) customers will bring you more work than the Yellow Pages or any kind of ad.

2. Keep your head in the toilet—stay on the job.
3. Specialize in an area that suits you (windows? floors? carpets? motel maid work? bank cleaning?)—and let everyone know what your specialty is.
4. Keep your overhead small. Don't worry about acting like a big businessperson. Hire cautiously and only if you have to. Operate out of a modest office and a used vehicle. Save money whenever you can—cleaning can't support high rolling.
5. Above all, use your own money. Borrowing, especially from friends or family, only gives you false security and inexperienced advisors, both bad.

Work hard and stick with it until you get good. You'll grow and prosper.

> For a complete, easy to understand, step-by-step guide to everything you ever need to know about the business, including model forms and contracts, get yourself a copy of *Cleaning Up For A Living* by Don Aslett and Mark Browning. You can learn a lot just from the pro cleaning chapter of *Is There Life After Housework!*

Don Aslett
Speaks Out

King of the Toilet Ring is also

King of the Podium

Don Aslett has delighted thousands of audiences with his humor and insight.

A veteran speaker, best-selling author, businessman, family man and media personality, Don is high on life and can mold any theme in to a power-packed message no one will forget. He is excellent on a wide variety of business and management topics as well as general morale-building—and any aspect of cleaning, home or professional. Whether speaking to doctors, lawyers, janitors, or the League of Women Voters, Don is a master at inspiring and motivating people.

In his nearly 200 days of in-person appearances each year, Don brings his homespun humor and down-to-the-bottomline message to everyone from homemakers to business executives to grade school assemblies—Alaska to Jacksonville, Florida. His clients include such groups as American Express, IBM, GTE, and NIKE.

> Here's a sampling of this year's calendar: Pizza Expo, Las Vegas • Big Island Resource Conservation and Development, Hawaii • Coast to Coast Convention, San Francisco • Vacuum Dealer Trade Association, Las Vegas • Minneapolis Home and Garden Show • Super 8 Motels International convention, New Orleans • Winnepeg Home Shows • Century 21, Jackson Hole • Executive Cleaning Show, Chicago • Simplot Soil Builders, Boise • Visalia Community Bank Employee Rally, California • Cotter Market, Chicago • Tacoma Home and Garden Show • Department of Human Services, Salt Lake City and MORE!

Rapid-fire presentation, fast-paced wit, action-packed demonstrations, new fun facts, and the ability to bring everyone to side-splitting laughter makes Don popular with the media as well as live audiences. Local and national show hosts welcome Don whenever he's in town.

It all began with...
Is There Life After Housework?

A three-hour course in pro cleaning short-cuts that Don first gave when his wife, Barbara, asked him to speak to her women's group at church. It was hard to answer all the questions that came up at the seminars, so he wrote them down and self-published the book *Is There Life After Housework?* It was picked up by Writer's Digest Books and went on to make the bestseller list. Since then Don has taught millions how to cut housework by 75% with his seminars, books and his video tape.

A newly expanded and revised tenth anniversary edition is hot off the presses adding all the wisdom Don has gleaned in the last ten years.

The topic of "housework" launched Don Aslett's speaking career, but the business savvy that turned the janitorial company he founded into a multi-million dollar national corporation makes him a perennial favorite of boardroom audiences. Some of his most popular presentations:

- •Clutter's Last Stand—don't let clutter and junk rob your most valuable commodity: time!
- •Building a success-minded attitude
- •How to be a more valuable employee
- •How to do a thousand things at once—effective time management
- •The bad logic of being average
- •From Outhouse to Penthouse (how Don made a million scrubbing toilets)
- •How you can turn even the dirtiest job into a gold mine

Even the time-worn topics of management, motivation, marketing, self-esteem, communication, ad infinitum take on a new life in Don's electric presentations. And he always leaves his listeners with things that they can take home and start using today—this minute, to improve their lives and their business careers.

He's made over 5000 appearances:

- Conventions
- Trade Shows
- Business Meetings
- Employee Training
- Keynote Addresses
- After Dinner Speeches
- Entertainment
- Partner Programs
- Program Emcee
- Panel Leader
- Church Group Programs
- Education In-service Groups
- Grade School Assemblies
- Rotary and other civic groups
- *Life After Housework* seminar on cleaning short-cuts

The heart of this man—his true calling—is his ability to motivate. How else could he have gotten millions of Americans to enjoy cleaning? Don Aslett inspires his listeners, viewers, and readers to get through the necessary chores more efficiently so they can get on with the things they really love and enjoy.

> **This is a sampling of what Don Aslett offers as a speaker, but if you submit your needs he can tailor a program around your theme.**
>
> **For current scheduling information, please call Tobi Haynes in Don's office at 208-232-6212.**

Got any old or unique cleaning equipment?

Don Aslett's Cleaning Museum would like to know about it. Call or write and let us know exactly what you have—it might be perfect to add to our collection.

We're interested in commercial as well as home cleaning gear of any kind—old vacuums, mops, washers, buckets, etc.—as well as old cleaning products and chemicals still in their original packaging. Keep us in mind if you come across old ads or signs for cleaning products, old books or brochures on cleaning, or photos or stories of great moments in cleaning history, too.

The Cleaning Museum, located right here at my headquarters in Pocatello, Idaho, is rapidly becoming the biggest and best anywhere—it's attracting worldwide as well as nationwide attention. Sell or donate that old artifact to us and help raise eyebrows, teach history, and build appreciation for the second oldest profession.

Please call if you have a unique item! And if you have a snapshot, drop it in the mail so we can tell if it's something we already have. And tell us how much you're willing to part with it for or if you'll donate the item.

208-232-6212

Don Aslett's Cleaning Museum
PO Box 700, Pocatello, ID 83204